indexed

Jessica Hagy

VIKING STUDIO

VIKING STUDIO
Published by the Penguin Group
Penguin Group (USA) Inc., 375 Hudson Street,
New York, New York 10014, U.S.A.
Penguin Group (Canada), 90 Eglinton Avenue East, Suite 700,
Toronto, Ontario, Canada M4P 2Y3
(a division of Pearson Penguin Canada Inc.)
Penguin Books Ltd, 80 Strand, London WC2R 0RL, England
Penguin Ireland, 25 St. Stephen's Green, Dublin 2, Ireland
(a division of Penguin Books Ltd)
Penguin Books Australia Ltd, 250 Camberwell Road, Camberwell,
Victoria 3124, Australia
(a division of Pearson Australia Group Pty Ltd)
Penguin Books India Pvt Ltd, 11 Community Centre, Panchsheel Park,
New Delhi – 110 017, India
Penguin Group (NZ), 67 Apollo Drive, Rosedale, North Shore 0632,
New Zealand (a division of Pearson New Zealand Ltd)
Penguin Books (South Africa) (Pty) Ltd, 24 Sturdee Avenue,
Rosebank, Johannesburg 2196, South Africa

Penguin Books Ltd, Registered Offices:
80 Strand, London WC2R 0RL, England

First published in 2008 by Viking Studio,
a member of Penguin Group (USA) Inc.

1 3 5 7 9 10 8 6 4 2

Copyright © Jessica Hagy, 2008
All rights reserved

ISBN 978-0-14-200520-0

Printed in the United States of America
Set in Times Ten • Designed by Alissa Amell

This seems like a good place to start.

A.

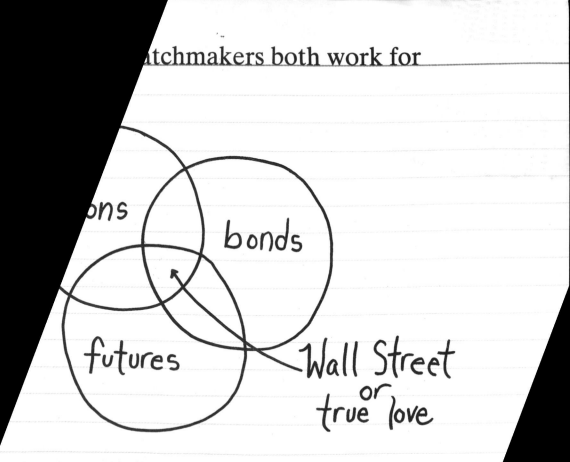

ons

bonds

futures

Wall Street
or
true love

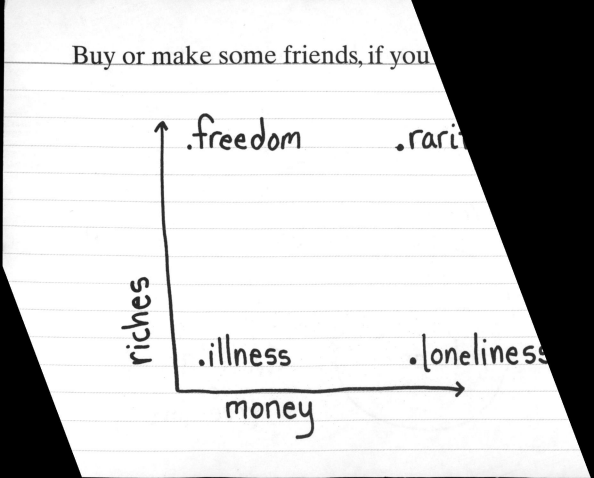

.freedom   .rari[t]

riches

.illness   .loneliness

money

you can't take it with you.

A = Become a vampire

B = Discover something magnificent

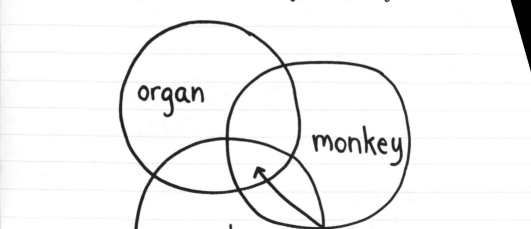

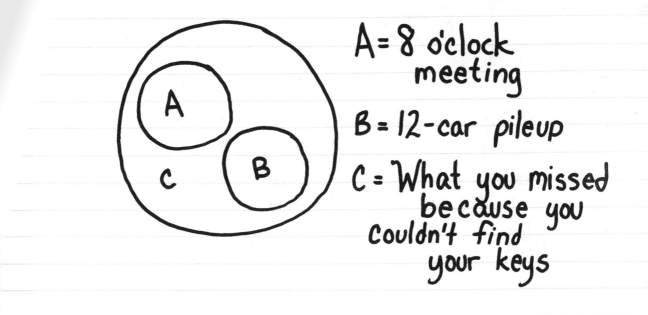

If your mouth's shut, your foot can't get in it.

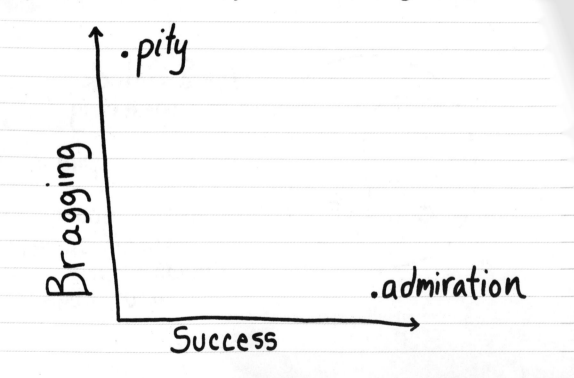

Don't believe the hype, especially if your mom wrote it.

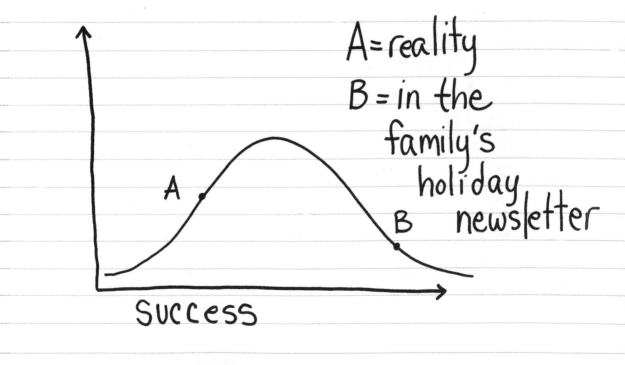

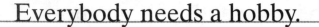
Everybody needs a hobby.

Guitar Sales

Ugly guys with cute girlfriends

A good haircut pays for itself.

If you can't play guitar, play the sympathy card.

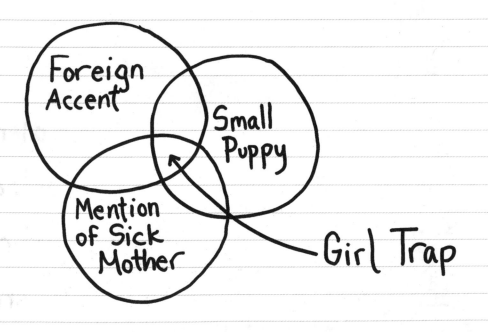

And keep your chin up, but not that far.

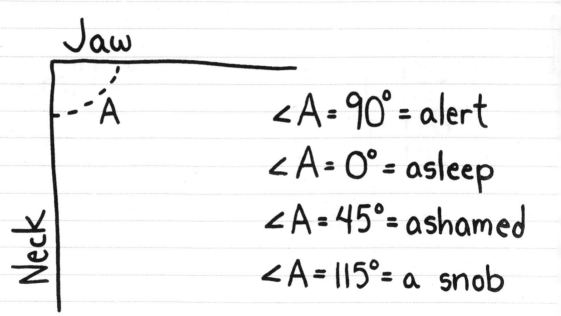

∠A = 90° = alert

∠A = 0° = asleep

∠A = 45° = ashamed

∠A = 115° = a snob

Like he reads any of them anyway.

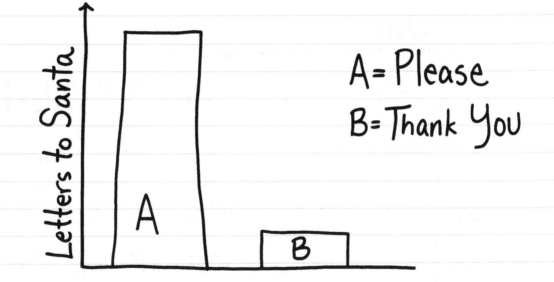

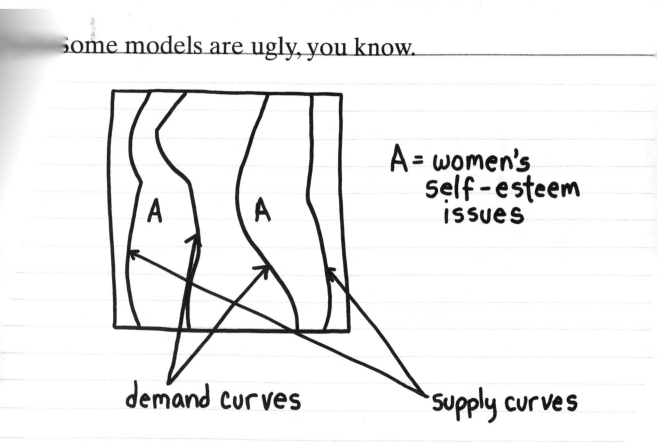

A = women's self-esteem issues

demand curves

supply curves

We can't get away with everything.

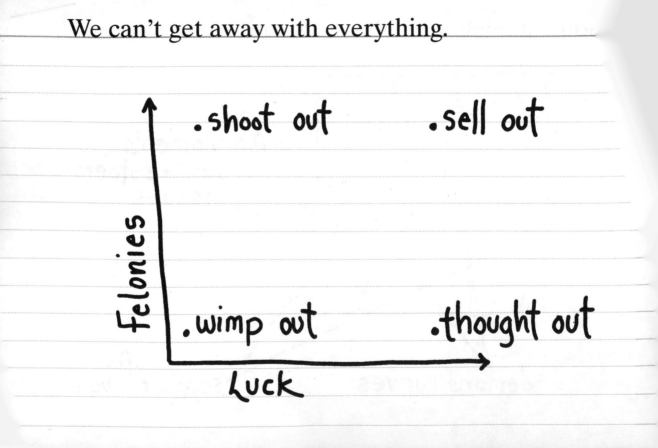

That's where the good lawyers come in.

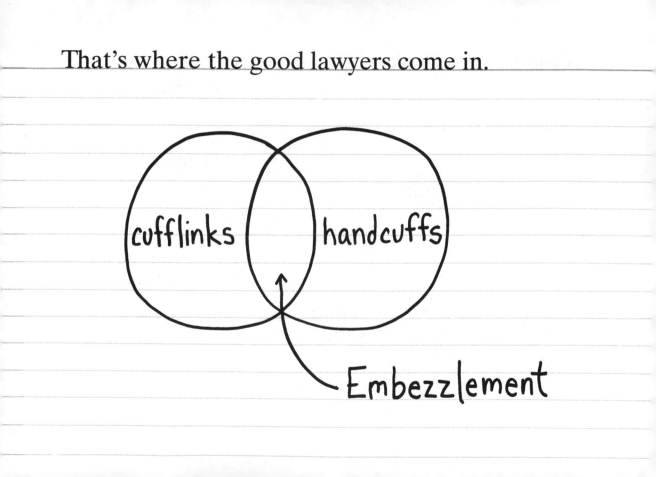

Is the system broken or just polluted?

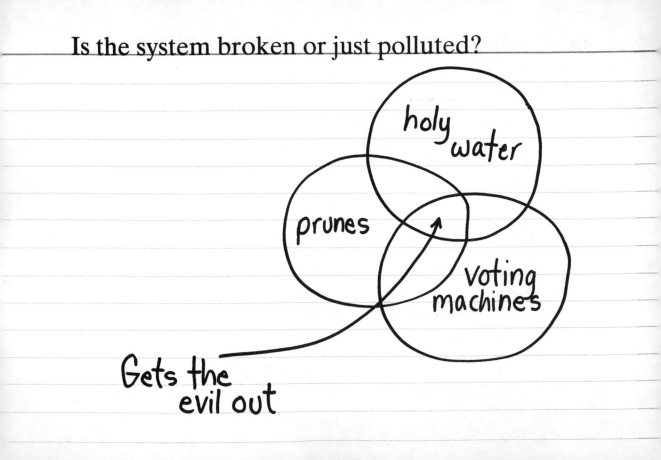

Either way, there's damned jewerly involved.

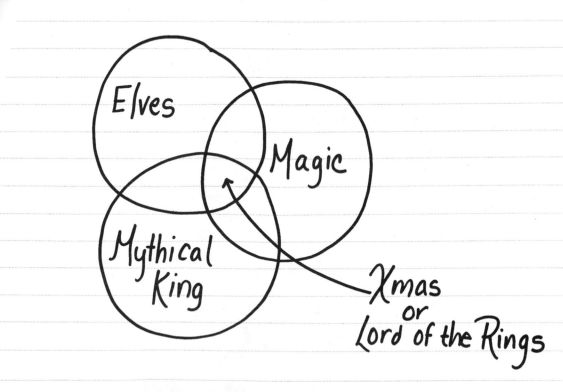

That's why he never gets the big piece of chicken

A = You play catch with Dad

B = Your redheaded brother does not

Everybody knows a story like that, in some way or another.

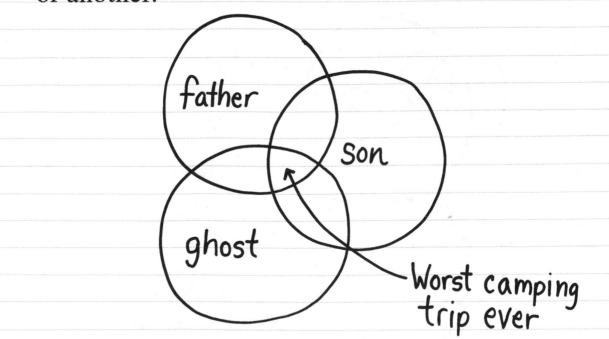

father

son

ghost

Worst camping trip ever

He doesn't have nine lives, either, though.

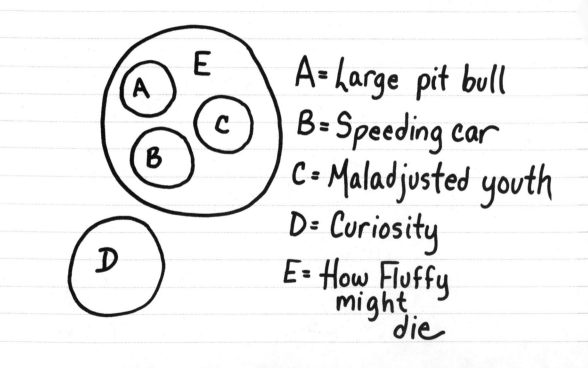

A = Large pit bull

B = Speeding car

C = Maladjusted youth

D = Curiosity

E = How Fluffy might die

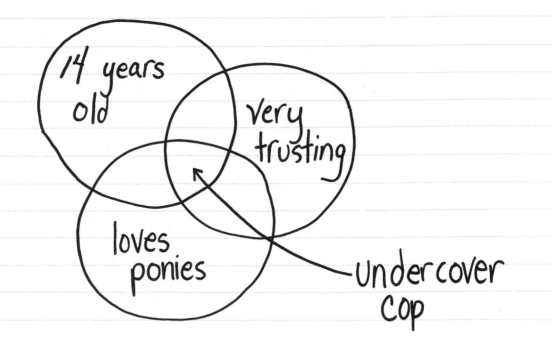

14 years old

very trusting

loves ponies

undercover cop

In a sitcom, the men are dumpy and the women are gorgeous. You don't live in a sitcom.

$x = brains$
$y = looks$

$A = him$

$B = you$

$C = your\ chance$

Why doesn't the dog bark when they visit?

Blessed or lucky, you still owe taxes on that.

Yes, you're special. Now give me my fries.

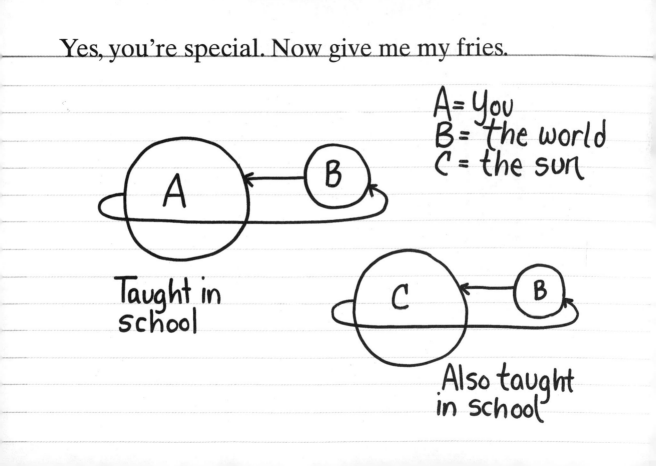

Some are compelled to nod, the rest just nod off.

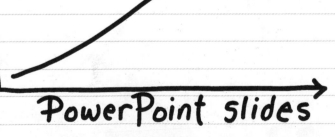
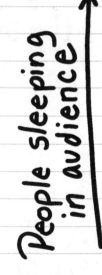

Ever feel like Lady Macbeth? You know, insane?

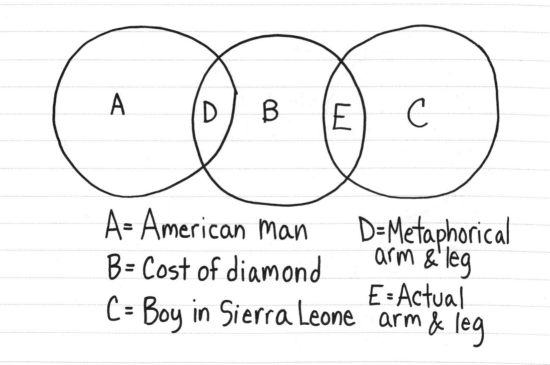

A = American Man

B = Cost of diamond

C = Boy in Sierra Leone

D = Metaphorical arm & leg

E = Actual arm & leg

Free refills? Not everywhere, sorry.

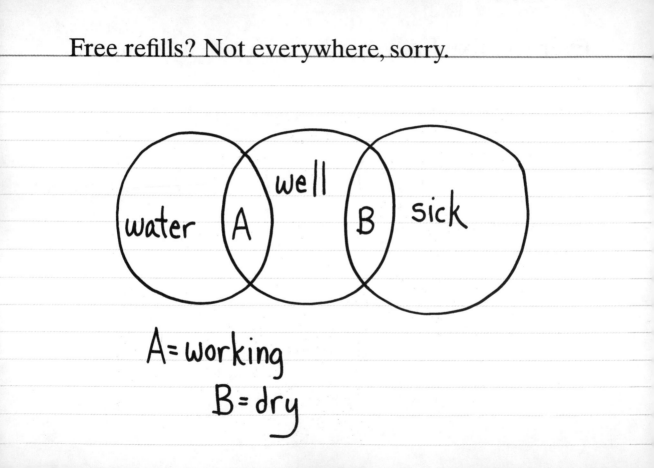

Watch the contortionist fit into this tiny cube!

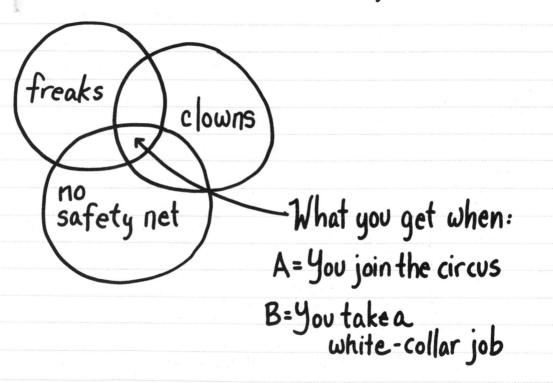

freaks

clowns

no
safety net

What you get when:

A = You join the circus

B = You take a
white-collar job

Quit making yourself miserable.

Cheers!

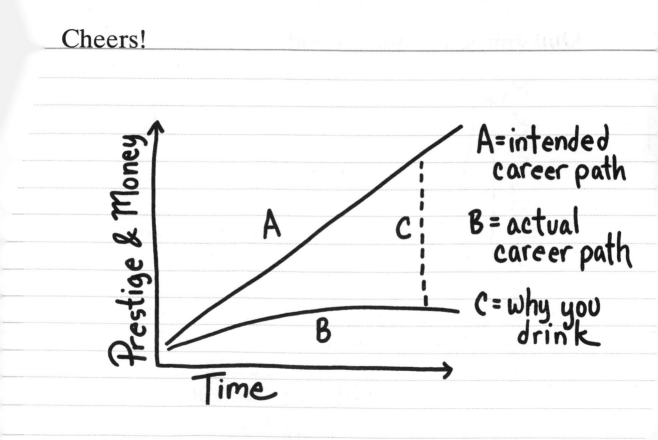

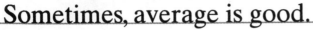

Sometimes, average is good.

How much others mock you (vertical axis)

How well you're doing (horizontal axis)

Average is left alone, too.

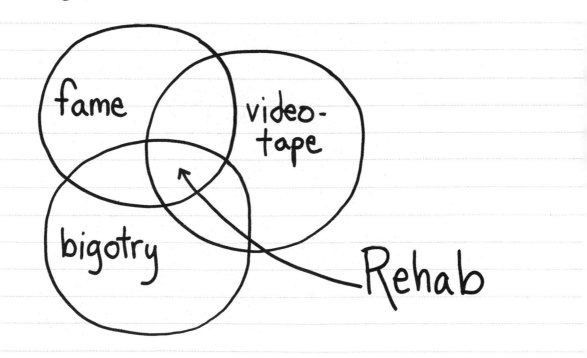

And that's how Mommy and Daddy met.

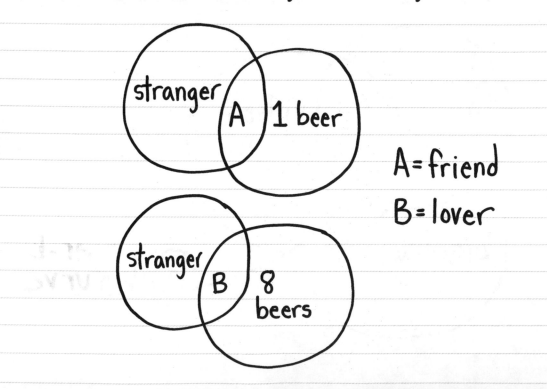

Volume to mass conversion is possible.

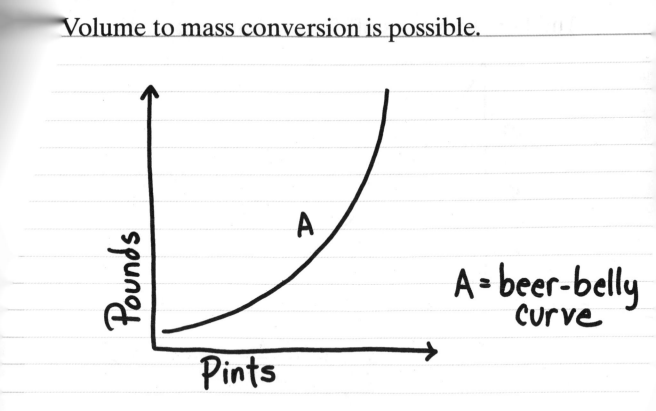

The novelty wears off faster than you think.

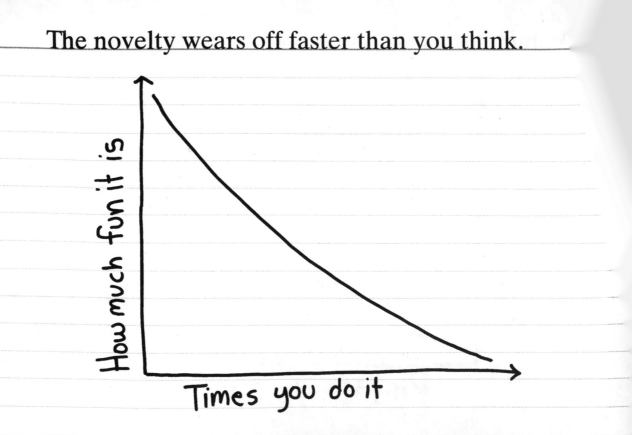

job market = entrepreneurship

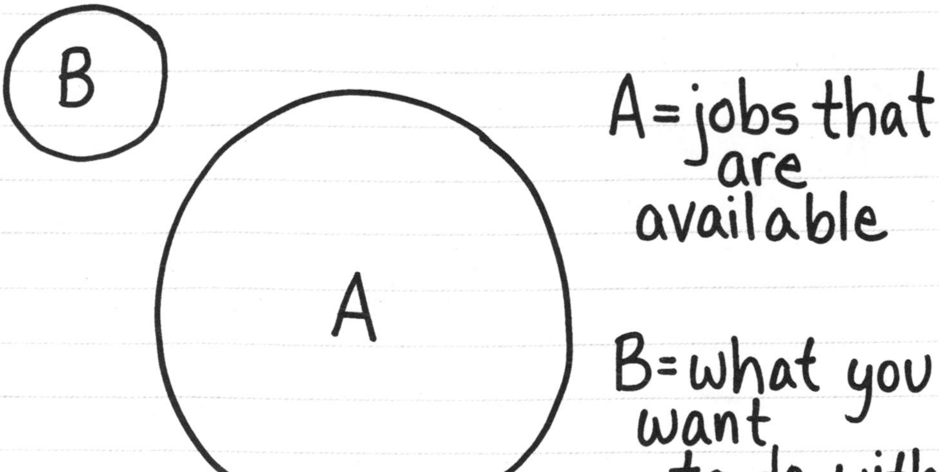

B

A

A = jobs that
are
available

B = what you
want

Being alone is better than being alone with wrong person.

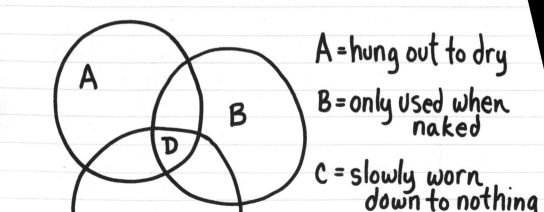

A = hung out to dry

B = only used when naked

C = slowly worn down to nothing

So place your bets.

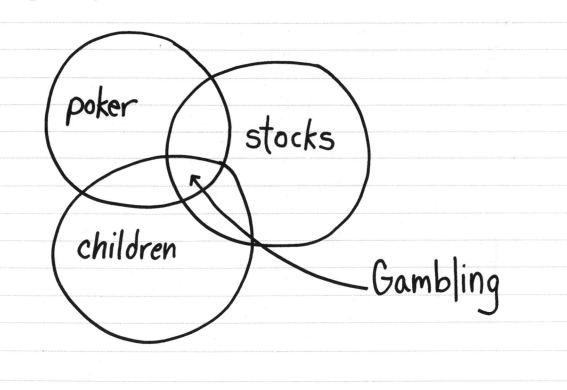

poker

stocks

children

Gambling

Do you remember what happened?

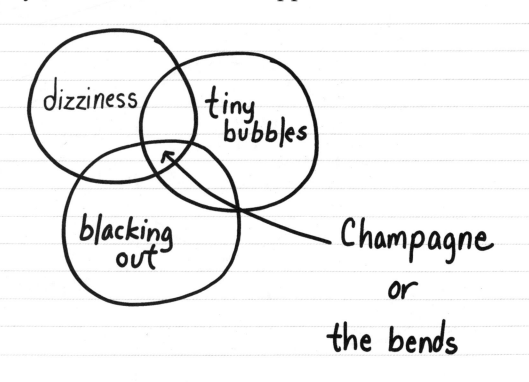

dizziness

tiny bubbles

blacking out

Champagne
or
the bends

At the stroke of midnight, indeed.

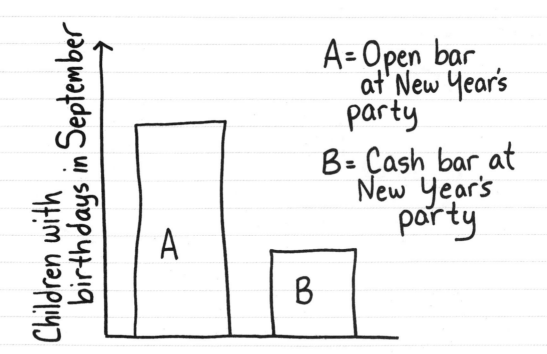

A = Open bar at New Year's party

B = Cash bar at New Year's party

Is "plays well with others" really so much
of a compliment?

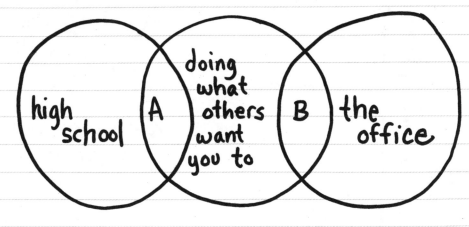

A = giving in to peer pressure
B = being a team player

Sharing: It keeps the anarchists away.

Are you in your element?

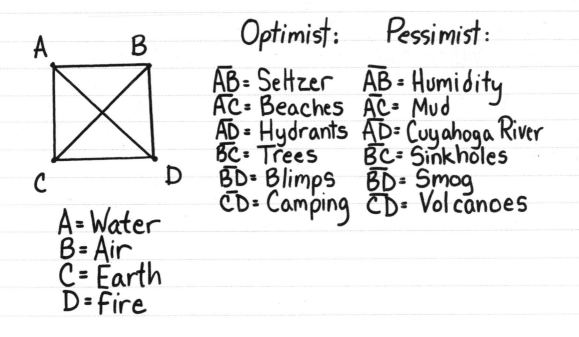

Optimist:
- $\overline{AB}$ = Seltzer
- $\overline{AC}$ = Beaches
- $\overline{AD}$ = Hydrants
- $\overline{BC}$ = Trees
- $\overline{BD}$ = Blimps
- $\overline{CD}$ = Camping

Pessimist:
- $\overline{AB}$ = Humidity
- $\overline{AC}$ = Mud
- $\overline{AD}$ = Cuyahoga River
- $\overline{BC}$ = Sinkholes
- $\overline{BD}$ = Smog
- $\overline{CD}$ = Volcanoes

A = Water
B = Air
C = Earth
D = Fire

Optimists apologize often.

Efficiency is just another word for a cheap
apartment.

Style is subjective.

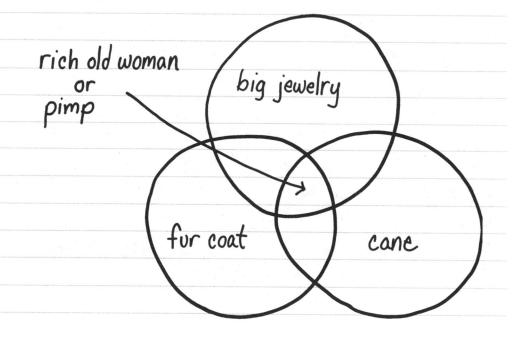

rich old woman
or
pimp

big jewelry

fur coat

cane

Yep, practically everything is subjective.

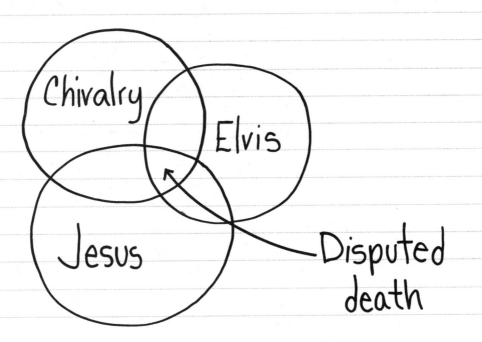

Chivalry

Elvis

Jesus

Disputed death

So don't believe everything you hear.

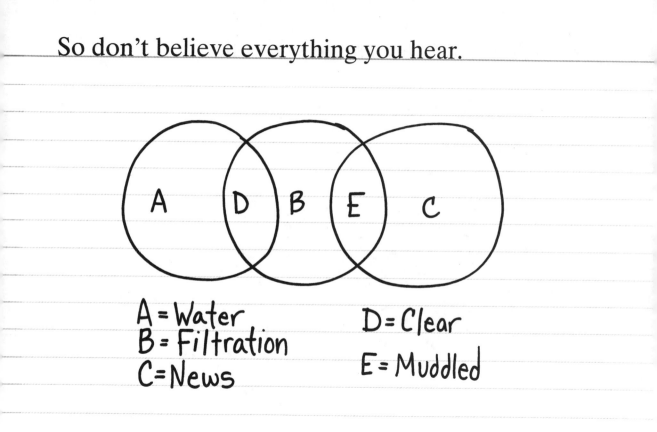

A = Water
B = Filtration
C = News

D = Clear
E = Muddled

Rorschach tests are made with ink.

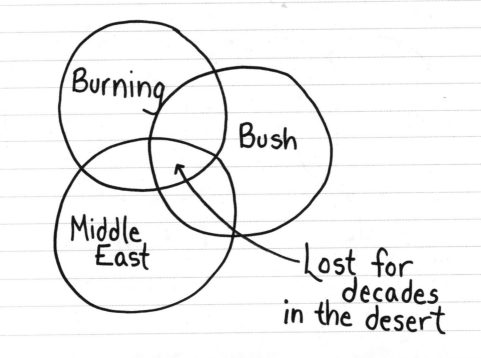

Burning

Bush

Middle
East

Lost for
decades
in the desert

Playing outside: suggested for both overweight kids and overwrought adults.

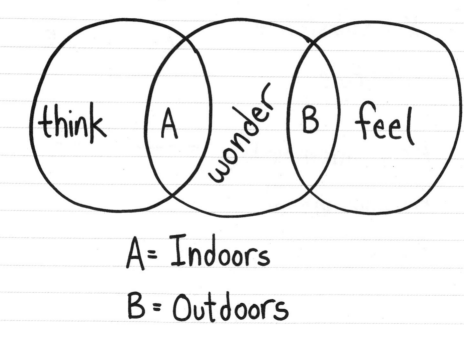

A = Indoors

B = Outdoors

All are malleable.

x = substance

y = style

A = fashion model

B = role model

C = modeling clay

D = cheese in a can

Try not to step on anybody on the way up.

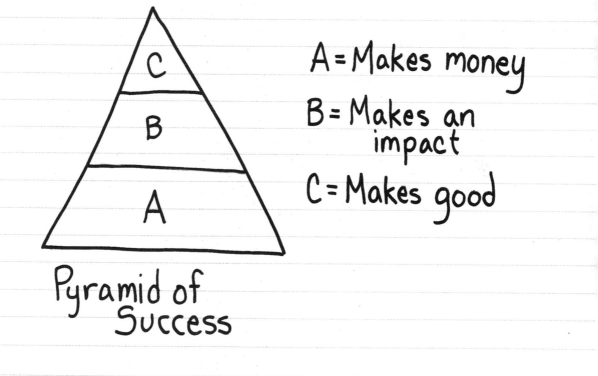

A = Makes money

B = Makes an impact

C = Makes good

Pyramid of Success

A   B

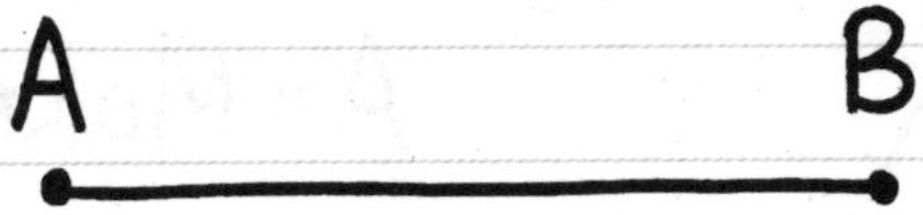

$A = $ ugly

$B = $ beautiful

$\vec{AB} = $ smile

$\vec{BA} = $ smirk

Misbehavior isn't always poor behavior.

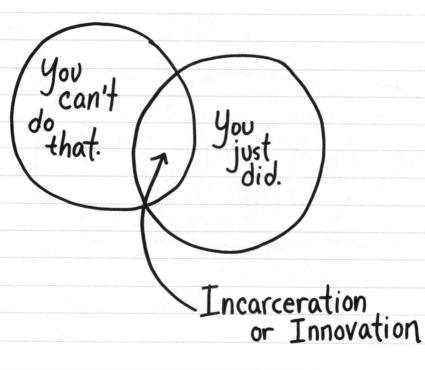

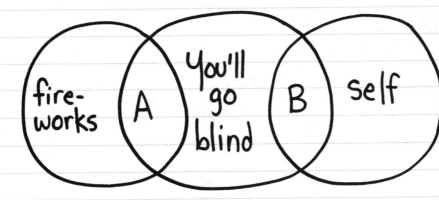

A = true   B = false

Did you hit your head on that wall again?

A = goldfish   C = worker
B = bowl   D = job

Girl, you know it's true.

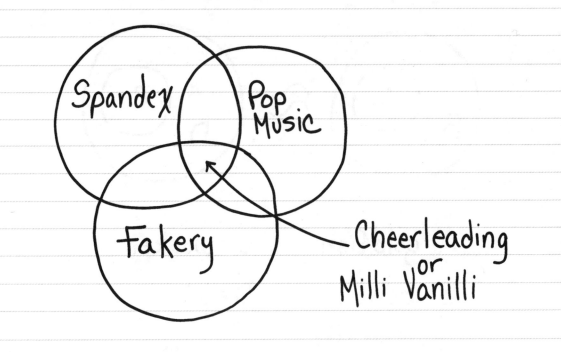

You know this is true as well.

Otherwise, you'll crash.

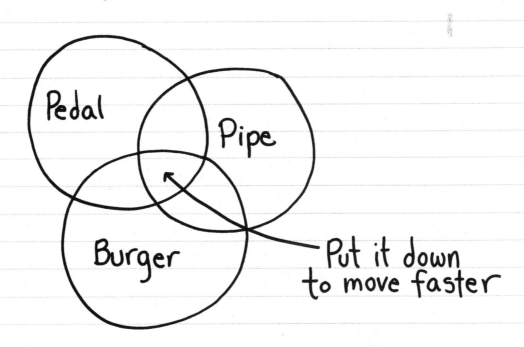

Just because you can eat it doesn't mean you should.

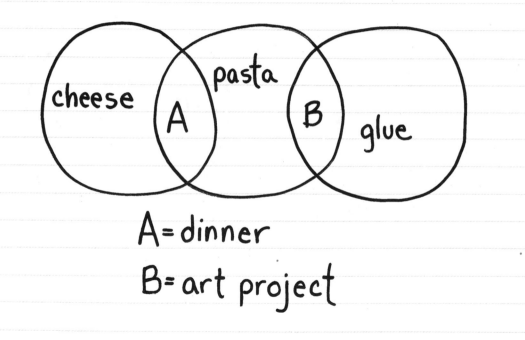

A = dinner

B = art project

There's no merit badge for surviving
emotional trauma.

A = hand of
     sleeping
     Cub Scout

B = bucket of
    warm water

B   A

Years of
  therapy

Don't play truth or dare with B. You will be shamed.

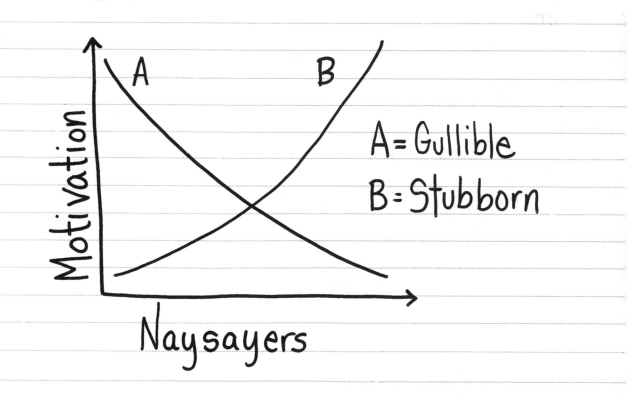

A = Gullible
B = Stubborn

I hear Vancouver's nice this time of year.

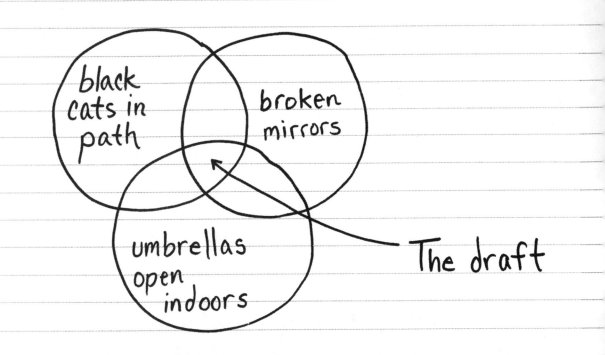

At least you inherited her flat feet.

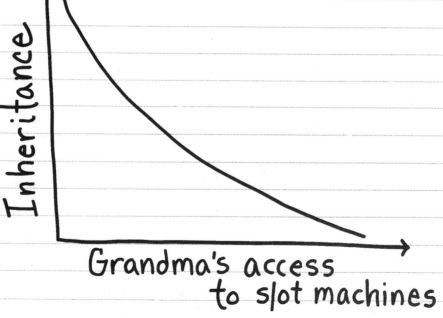

Inheritance

Grandma's access to slot machines

Sportsmanship = winners don't look smug and losers don't look bitter.

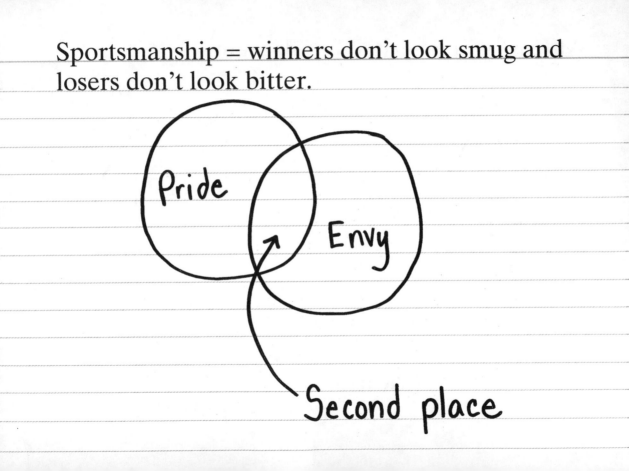

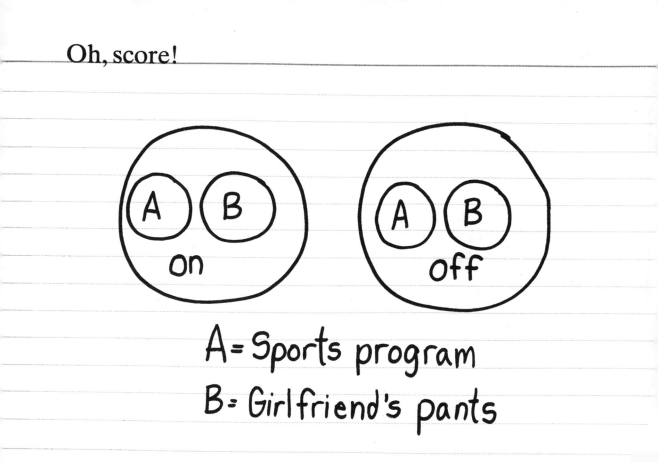

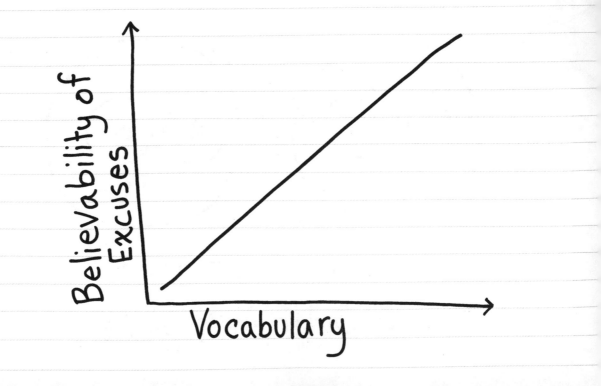

Go looking for trouble and you'll find it.

thickness of dictionary

Fate is pretty tempting.

But then most things that aren't good for you are rather appealing.

Sometimes you get more than you pay for.

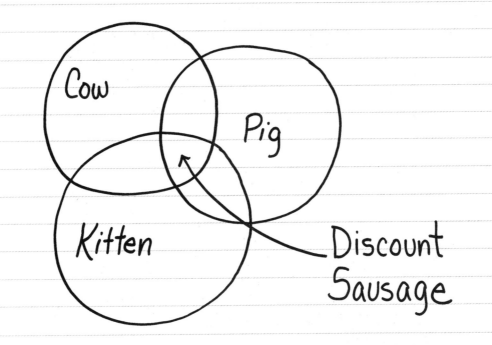

Ground chuck.

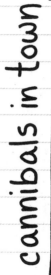

cannibals in town

fingers on local butcher

10

Just put some ketchup on it.

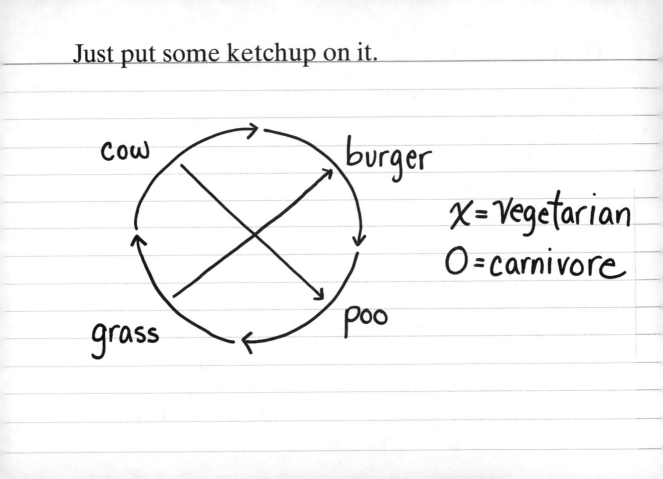

The road forks at every step.

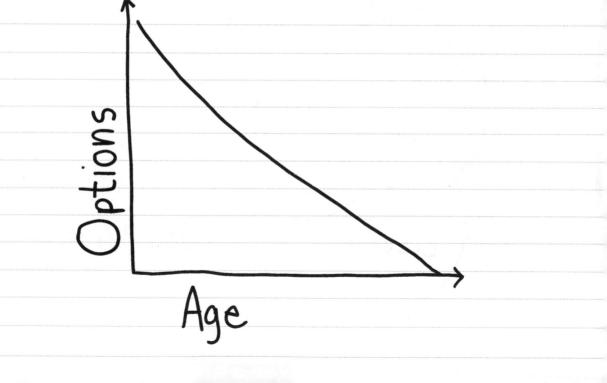

Shhh! I hear Mom coming—she's only a
block away.

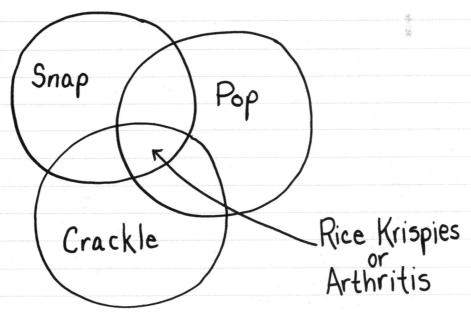

Either way, you're unemployed.

We all know who gets the girl.

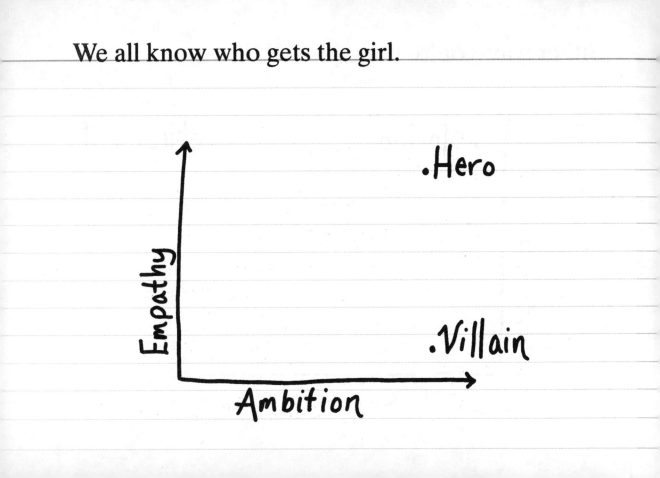

Honey, let's move to the suburbs.

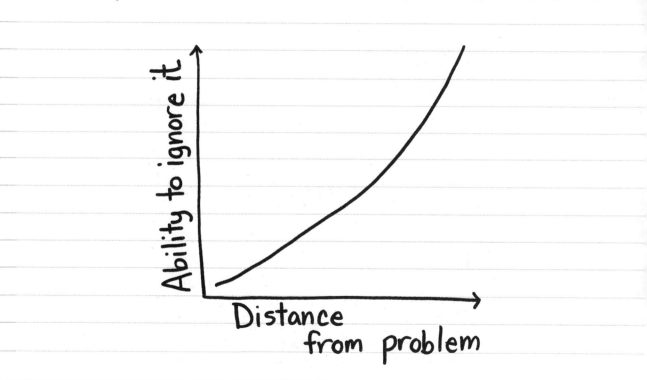

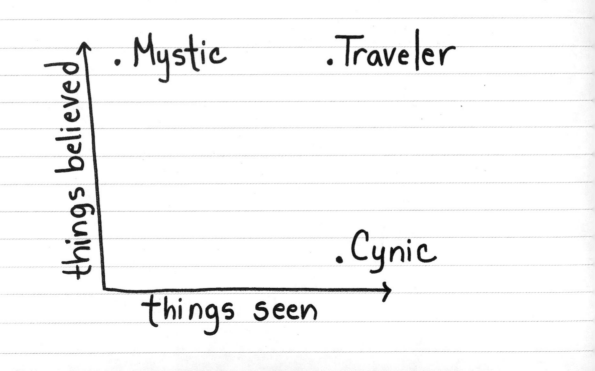

About those vacation days you keep forfeiting:

You're not from around here, are you?

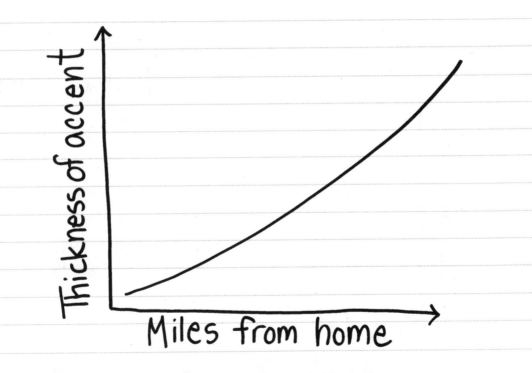

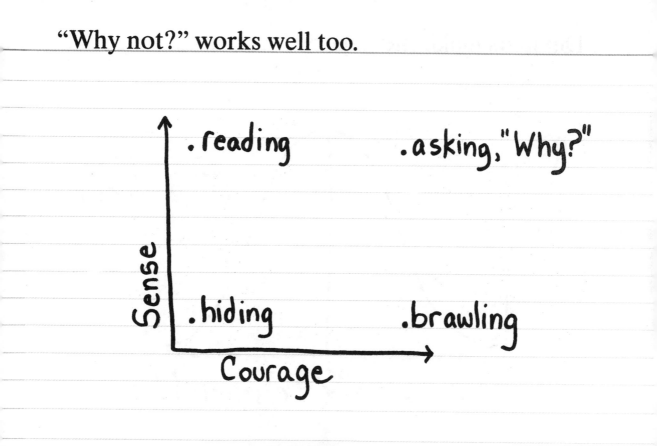

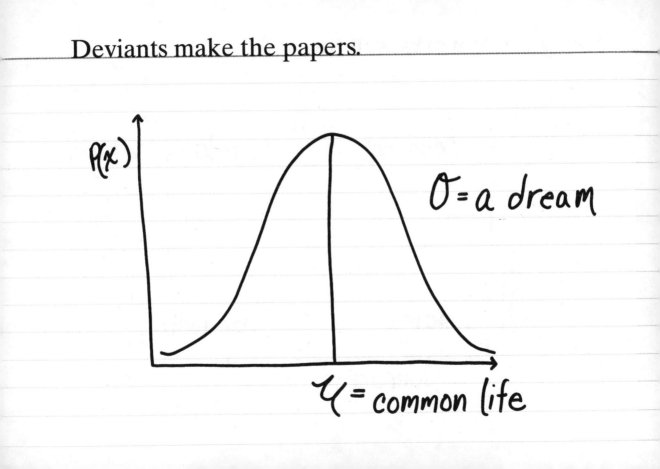

Do you want some sympathy or a solution?

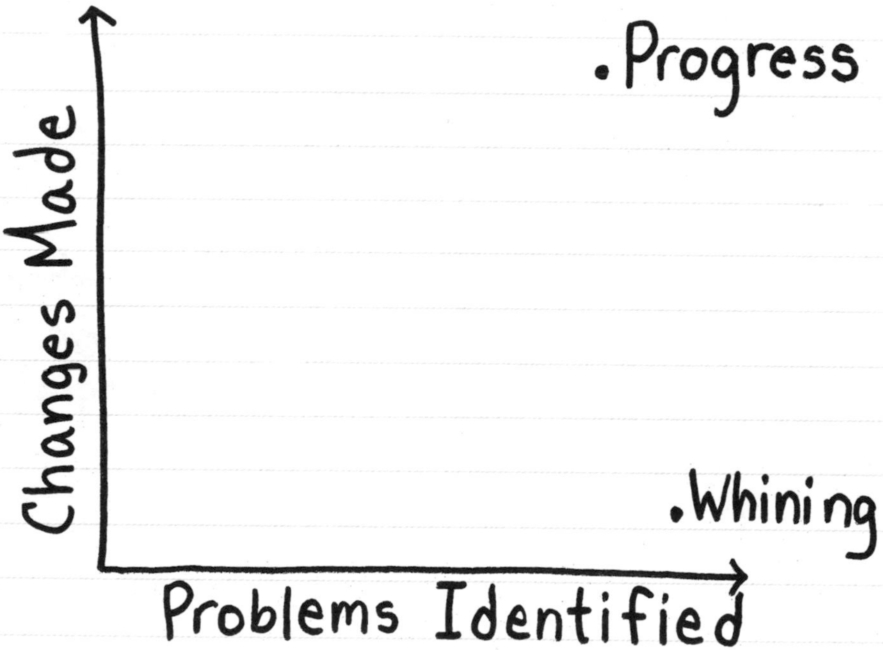

Changes Made

Progress

Whining

Problems Identified

Stop it? That's impossible.

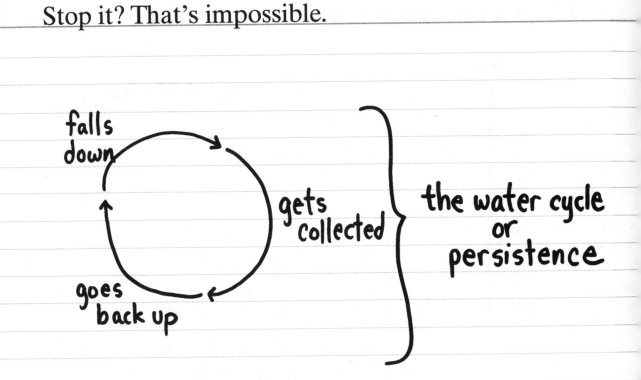

The revolution will not be sponsored by a brand-name antidepressant.

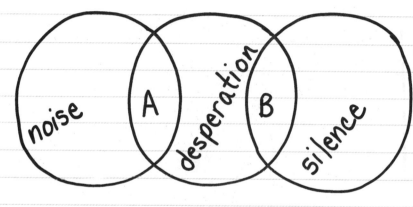

noise   A   desperation   B   silence

A = Uprising
B = Depression

I heard I had fun.

Memories of Party

1   21   101

Candles on Cake

We'll all change the world, somehow.

But what we leave behind is open
to interpretation.

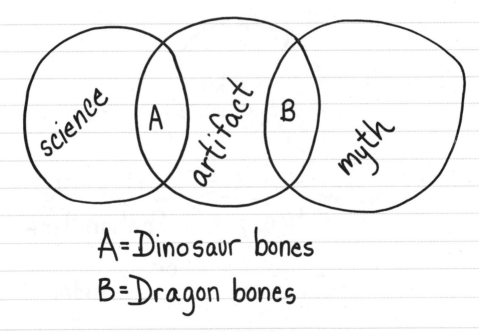

A = Dinosaur bones
B = Dragon bones

And one final point:

B.